DESERT CENTER

For more information:
Stephen F. Austin State University Press
P.O. Box 13007 SFA Station
Nacogdoches, Texas 75962
sfapress@sfasu.edu
www.sfasu.edu/sfapress

Book design: Tinesha Mix
Cover design: Tinesha Mix
Cover art: Bart Vargas, *Mandala 9*
Distributed by Texas A&M Consortium
www.tamupress.com

Excerpt from "Requiem for Sonora" from *Of All the Dirty Words*, by Richard Shelton, © 1972. Reprinted by permission of the University of Pittsburgh Press.

LIBRARY OF CONGRESS CATALOGING-IN-PUBLICATION DATA
Waggener, Miles
Desert Center / Miles Waggener
p.cm.

ISBN: 978-1-62288-158-1

DESERT CENTER

FLOATING MOTELS

FEVERSCAPE

DERRINGER

"...and to the dark shapes it touches
searching for what it has not lost
and will never find
searching
and lonelier
than even I can imagine"

> —Richard Shelton
> from "Requiem for Sonora"

Desert Center

Sonoran Namazu

Where were you born, butter cat? Dive down
with weighted gizzard. From what crack in the earth
did your naked, twitching body wake
to break open this desert shell? Fovea, divot—
where you track and hang the horned owl
to the back of your head like a camera obscura—
is cloudless, burning, and hasn't had rain
in a thousand days. Arroyos, coughing with sleepers,
dream off the heat of onramps, spillways, home.
What need have eyes or owls when you hunt
by taste, expanding mouth, no incisiform teeth,
suctioning slack current behind dredge spoils, in slime
gathering in channels, growing monstrous
in the deepest scour holes? Leave bad news
to the fleeing owl, sinker line your
eye draws down the middle of a fissure, tectonic
fault filled with canal water and moonlight
refracted as you wake. Wake up, stinging halo
burning through fans of ether, turning chapters
of algae among rusty debris. Like an owl, you
hunt in the dark. Let me shine a light into your
whiskered face, your tinny shallows of eye-glow,
bright veil, tapetum lucidum capturing
photons in the silt. You're waiting for me,
catfish, bringer of earthquakes, still dreaming
our aging dead, murk of not a soul,
light of shattering bulb, my shiny lure.

You Must Drive to Phoenix

I'm sorry. Turn off your air conditioner. I know
it's humid and the drivers are angry. Roll down
a window, take your phone
and throw it into a canal. Satellites won't
help you now. There is a way to understand
one wild secret: I'm asking you to sleep

in a vacant lot in the center
of a city. To rest on the belly of wilderness,
you have to lie on bull-head thorns that poke
through a dead softball diamond. Find a field

where cotton and alfalfa won't
grow, no matter how much water
is pressed down upon them. Only a backstop
twists and rusts where sports and grass
failed. In a hall of the San Carlos Hotel, refer
to an aerial picture of this place. It shows
the faintly dug creases of the Hohokam who
grew corn and tepary beans. You must sleep
where their water wouldn't cross, a small dry
square between mountains. Canals still give
it a wide berth. Cattle tear their hides in
cat-claw acacia at the shake of a rattle. You have

only a rusty backstop and a raggedy
pomegranate tree to go on, but don't sleep
near these characters. They are bad
companions, false ambassadors, visitors
like yourself. They have worn their welcome
to rust and tattered fruit. Ants make better
bed fellows. Watch the swifts

perch in the holes when the metal cools
at dusk. An elf owl will make a racket
blinking in the branches of moon-lit, gutted

pomegranates. Along an avenue, park
and lose your hubcaps. Leave your car unlocked,
and into a row of dead trees enter.

Tire Fire

The lot beside the re-upholstery shop,
a few doors down (if you can call
barbed wire fences doors) from Peaches
Live Girl Review on Cave Creek Road,
is on fire. All week, the words *suspected*
and *arson* appear together in the mouths
of anchor persons. Blame cigarettes, the match
in mid-July, or blame the owner of the lot
who lives in San Diego, who no one
has ever seen. Blame sunlight flashing
on every ditched car beside the metal fence
mounted with orphaned hubcaps
and bulging with tires, and blame the ten-year-old
newly-minted Jesus freak (me), who is in love
with the tire fire. He rides his bike to the road
blocked by emergency vehicles and wants
to experience firsthand the asphalt-buckling
heat against his face. How inevitable
a tire fire feels when it happens. A tire won't burn
below 400°. But blame the pivot of a boot
at the wrong time. Or the city of car batteries
buried in oily dirt. Blame bad thoughts and the crumbs,
which he learns are bits of rubber that can
self-ignite. There's television footage
of his neighborhood, and of volcanoes,
and Titan missiles poised beneath the desert,
and the crucible of souls he's convinced
is destined for America. He has to get as close
as he can to such heat and shake his head
at his brother who says holy fuck
as they watch the unbraiding rope
of smoke filmed from helicopters they
hear overhead. The boy peddles
to staging areas where men bend their bodies
into the straps of heavy equipment
to protect themselves from valves of hot fluid

shooting from the televised event.
Blame the plastic hubcaps with crests of fiery birds
contracting like poisoned spiders inside the boy's dreams,
as carbon monoxide, sulfur dioxide, styrene,
butadiene flow freely from a flaming cresset,
laying bare before all with eyes that might see
the backs of freshly laid carpet,
roofing materials, auto parts, the pissy foam
beneath the old dog who also dreams
but has no soul. Blame the very food in its mouth,
that we may know well what the fallen world is made of,
and that it can, with little coaxing, catch flame
and burn forever.

Dirt Bike

J. rides his dirt bike
the length of desert
counties to take the keys
from the half of Arizona
that can't pay. There are fish
hooks hung at eye level
and meth labs. I don't creep up
on them anymore,
he tells me, banking the five
ball off the rail. But I try
to work at night, so I can
get back here by happy hour.
They hear me coming.
I bet I've played thirty
games of pool with J.,
but I've never heard him
speak so many words.
I've never seen him turn
his head either. That's my beer.
He's looking down his cue
at the eight ball. Yours is
over there. His peripheral
vision is flawless, his glasses
thick and dusty. Head
shaved to blonde gray shadow.
Smaller banks hire me.
Lots of trailer parks,
manufactured homes.
Unincorporated places like
Wintersberg, near the nuclear plant.
He rides his route all night
into morning, eats at the breakfast
counter at the Dinner Bell,
and comes here by four.
When I ask about guns
and dogs, he says they're

mostly vacated by the time
the bank calls him. But yes,
people breed pit bulls
in Wintersberg. When he says he
keeps the humane society and
animal control in his phone, I
stop myself short of asking
about child protective services.
But I'm feeling smug asking J.
all these questions. We're so
different, but united in this
pool game. He's not exaggerating.
He's beating me. I'm going to
buy him a beer. No, he was never
a private detective, and he doesn't
serve papers for lawyers. I just
take keys and hang lockboxes
on knobs. He walks through
the empty units to make sure
they're empty. He has a flashlight.
His boots crunch flies on linoleum,
his boots part seas of dust and hair.
Tweakers are the worst, he says
after a pause. They're up all night
taking things apart: hot water
heaters, copper plumbing,
cars, stoves, the voice chips inside
stuffed dolphins that talk to you.
But that's not my problem.
No one's ever surprised to see me.
When I push my coins in
and the pool balls drop,
I tell myself I'll ask him. I'll ask J.
if he likes his job. But soon
the balls are racked tight
in their triangle, the bathroom
is empty, there are two beers sweating
on the table, and I've been waiting for
him to come back
from his smoke for a long time.

Off-Track Betting

A racehorse tumbles, crushing its tiny
Jockey, and no one in the bar makes a sound.
Think horse head pressed flat into muddy ground,
Clouds and cameras in its eye, think motley
Sleeve, wrist bones of a child in silks. Every
Room locks behind you, feels booby-trapped.
Something is happening, you're a moon trapped
In a barred window of the county
Courthouse. You turn to the stranger beside you
To find out exactly what you are to feel
But his face is a drawer of useless keys
And the horse is still breathing. You don't know what you
Feel. Then they play it back for you: a racehorse
Tumbles, crushing its tiny jockey...

Creative Nonfiction

Black leaves, muddy ground, quiet thorny brambles
Around Northrop Grumman's high security fence at 3 a.m.,
Grass worn away, polished by halogen and boots
Of a weary watchman dreaming of his unfinished
Science fiction novel in which he orbits around
The high security planet that does something
He has yet to figure out, but he's thinking about it
As he looks at the facility under his watch, how exit signs
At intervals along the fire escapes look like a ladder up
To Venus. And there's a freshwater lake on the planet he
Doesn't understand, with a trillionaire's exact replica
Of a tiny marina of aluminum masts on Saguaro Lake.
That the planet is uninhabited helps the trillionaire sleep better.
Some nights the watchman thinks of the online
Creative writing degree he got from a school in Florida.
His dissertation, a handsomely bound thirty-seven page volume of
A prospectus of his science fiction novel called *The Secret Planet*
Of Arizona, was praised by its chair, a bestselling author who
Has to use an alias to protect his or her famous identity.
The watchman spends a lot of time at bookstores
Wondering which bestseller is his teacher, his secret mentor, whose
One suggestion was that he should call it a memoir,
Which he did in order to graduate. His two free copies
Included with his tuition have yet to arrive.

Grooming

Well into the hairdresser's
nervous breakdown, she snapped
the smock around my neck, and in
locks and curls, the hair, more hair
than I have grown in many lifetimes,
fell onto the tiles, and I grew thin
in the oily hum of the clippers,
in the perfume of tattooed Carlotta.
The salon lights cut in and out, but the razor
went on, and I had my haircut
into the dawn, the small engine
in her hand smoking, and she
was laughing, like a sheep, she
kept saying to me and didn't stop
for a smoke break. Generations of
aunties slinked out from beneath
their drier eggs, women with
strips of foil still in their hair
gave me a worried look, then
walked to their sedans. No one
rescued me. I looked for myself
in the streetlights reflected
there in the mirrors of the
abandoned bays. Almost
done, she said, but the razor
went against the grain of me,
and the dome of my head
bobbled in her grip as I resisted
sleep, and before I knew it, she
held a small mirror before me,
and there was a stranger
inside it vaguely resembling
a man nowhere even close
to being done.

The Academic

When his dead father called him
boy in a dream he woke up
and made coffee, thinking distantly of
doing what he loved all his life,
looking at the lights of his neighbors,
dabs of yellow bleaching to daylight
as they coated children or
left for work. Water ran in the sink
and he realized then he'd
been lying to himself. The ease
with which his teachers slipped
from one uncluttered surface
to another. How they praised him.
But the pleasures of really knowing
anything, where were they now?
Returning to the cup, spoon in hand, he
found his cup already held a spoon.
Students and librarians kept
telling him what he couldn't
remember. Enrollment low,
parking structures full, the school
where he taught was running out of room.
Later that night, with the stars behind
branches, he tried to remember a word
he couldn't summon—talisman.
As he propped himself against
a wire fence to think a minute,
he said the word—*fetish*. But
you mean *talisman*. The word
you want is *talisman*.

I Said David

I remember seeing a playing card
face down in a puddle of motor oil.
I said David don't touch it, that's
your card. And that's when I snitched.
There are only four people in the world
alive right now and I said David you are
one of them. The family doesn't let people
like me drive away and grow tomatoes.
I talk to high schools all the time.
Am I proud I sent a girl to jail? Was it
because she was a girl? I said David
she was a small link on a bigger chain. Am I
proud of this? no I am not. You tell me
why my cables were loose on that battery?
I said David, your life's a mess, a rat trap,
put paint on it, everything behind it
falls away. I talk to schools all the time.
You can't quit my job and leave no note.
Am I a dog person? No I am not
and that's okay. I can like other people's animals
from over here. You can't just turn a key
and drive. Motels, Gallup, New Mexico, Texas
panhandles look you right in the eye
when you leave the family. Like my
wife's sandals? They're peekaboo bunny.
You don't make eye contact with Idaho.
Schools ask me to talk to them all the time.
My wife says life's a bag of gummy
dicks—and that is why I love her.
I tell schools, next time you're at the zoo,
take a picture of an animal that will kill you.
Then take a second picture of an animal
that will not kill you. Take your pictures
home with you and look at your animals.
Can you tell the difference? No you cannot.
Not if you're David. Not if you're me.

Easter Island

To the stone faces without trees,
next to their long fields of shadow,
our shore party must look
like a chattering carpet
of camera flashes. The bird men
keep their heads in the wheeling constellations,
their arms by their stony sides,
their cold reasons beyond us,
their mouths shut.
Once I watched a toddler
waddle up to a tethered German shepherd:
the dog's still muzzle, the white control
of its eyes. The child's two hands,
tugged and tried the whiskers and
stiletto ears. Fat and drunk
from the cruise ship's club, we
pose against the wind-eaten cheeks
and bring our hands to the
lips of the shorter ones leaning
in the grass. I raise my fingers
to the wind-pocked noses,
as if they could sense
that we might wait one day
with a dead island beneath us,
our sky of answers out of reach,
like fruit ripening high in the trees.

Spirit

We were believers then
and we were penetrated by a ghost
even as our youth group turned
into ghosts, some by flames others
by the irradiating scenarios
of the handsome preacher, who
didn't look much older than us, but was
only giving us what we begged him for:
a primer on the end of the world,
that revelation we would see
in our lifetime. His wife wore a
low-cut sweater and led music.
Not a one of us, he promised,
would survive it, and our neurons scattered
like a Xerox of a Xerox skull he
showed us. We laughed at its
gangly caricature until he
started preaching again.
After it was all over there was nothing
like the school parking lot at night,
lustrous in the one working
headlight of Patrick's
station wagon. My friend Patrick—
whose baseball caps would be
lined up neatly alongside his open
casket by spring— would have
another surgery that week, and he
kept saying, Miles I'll go
when I'm called. I wasn't listening
but I remember my confusion
and fear about the end of the world,
and the pastor's wife who
changed the transparencies
of praise songs, her skin yellow in the light
of the overhead projector, words
we had just finished singing
for all the life in us sliding
across her neck and ear.

Nocturne

Concrete bends at the park's edge where halide lamps burnish wet leaves,
and a rattling orange osage spray painted for removal bears its torn page,
black sharpie letters that read *lost*

> *photograph vintage*
> *cardstock backing unframed*
> *if found please...*

1996

The swamp cooler breathes hot rust and spores
onto the polyester bedspread
my brothers and I vomited on as children.
A green phone mounts the wall
of mother's duplex where I have moved back in
now that I won't teach another year
of high school on the asteroid.
Through broken blinds
basalt breaks through a yellow mountain
once dotted with tuberculosis
patients coughing in tents before Phoenix was Phoenix.
With three college degrees, I must age
my seventy-year-old mother who knew
her son's truck of cassettes and jaundiced textbooks
was bound to roll up.
When she finally goes to bed,
night on the patio brings alarms
of not-so-distant burglary and boat-tailed grackles
who rasp like walkie-talkies
left on too long in the sweltering room
of this failure everyone saw coming
but me. Eventually, I creep back inside
to flip channels, where naked
bodies look nothing like naked bodies
but I don't care.
By noon, in exercise regalia, she waters
calla lilies, says there's cantaloupe
sliced up inside if I want it,
and because she won't ask me if I have a plan
I better tell us both something.

FLOATING MOTELS

Motel Window

Two sheriff's cars in halogen and snow
are slowly turning to gray lint
in the parking lot, as empty
as the tapping metal of central heat
and elevator door opening all night
for a coffee stain on beige carpet.
South Dakota winter opens as a ditch
of black ice we drove, misnamed
interstate, unscathed by salt and lethal
in its bend to Brookings. In the other bed
my three-year-old son is clutching
a plush dog he's named sister, eyes
trained on me, a stranger at the window
who brought us this far. My father
couldn't see summer as he slept
through it, 113 degrees decades ago,
in a room like this one, another season
in a motor lodge where I watched
his chest rise and fall. Granite
mountains outside memory seethed
behind eyelids closed by bourbon,
where we drove for no destination
up switchbacks that seemed to
buttonhook into himself as he smoked,
windows up. Hold on boy—
I still hear him. The truck cab
reeked of diesel and puke, floor mats
thrown out at a rest stop. But he is sleeping
in the second bed, safe from dangerous roads
that end in rooms we must share
the rest of our lives, or as long as memory
disinters motels. Or does it
bury them again like patrol cars in the snow,
their light bars abandoned luggage on top
where strangers slam their doors and drive away.

Night Work

On the bus ride home tonight an unsolicited hymn
assays us like plastic gold buttons as I take your hand to rise
from our seat. A woman's walker falls across the isle,
so we step over and away from the bubbly words
sung by evangelical passengers, the song about the father
being the potter, while you and I— late-middle-aged
father and small adopted son—we are the clay,
the work of his hands. In the ambulance light
of tree branches and poles, our big windows
sprayed with dried mud are also the work of his hands.
And there's nothing left to do but find your lost
rubber fireman boot wrapped in duct tape
mealy from slush and grime and put it back on.
What sea so wretched, I am dying to ask
no one but the night, puts this moment's foam
at our door? If there be but an onion skin between
my feelings and these passengers who step down
from chemical light to dissolve into the streets like tablets
how am I to feel them? We slip in and out of the cones
of streetlight and silence. Is this when you'll ask me again
where is god if I can't see him? Please not now.

Minimart

The woman in the checkout line in front of you
has her hand on the sun-bleached hair of a boy
of about nine. Plastic jug of milk
by the register. With a bouquet of beef jerky in your fist,
adolescence flickers and vanishes beneath buzzing
minimart halogen, black algae of childhood
blooming in the murky shallow end
of a swimming pool after your father died.
The plaster water bubble over the bed
when the roof leaked, dirty water graying
the wallpaper, that hot Phoenix summer your mother
bought two goats, Bob and Ray, to eat the weeds
that grew brittle and inedible. Bob was lanky, white,
his underbelly yellow with pee. Ray was half Bob's size,
coat and eyes the color of dry pinto beans.
Your mother grieved and held the little goat's head
in both hands, gazed into Ray's eyes, and
called him Darling Ray. They pulled out their stakes,
ate the weather stripping off the doors
until the doors opened, then dragged their tethers
and turds through the house. With air conditioner groaning, you
came home from school to an open front door,
curtain rod pulled down, Darling Ray tap-dancing
on the kitchen table, Bob in your closet chewing
the elastic out of your underwear. One afternoon,
Darling Ray, tether in tow, tried to jump over a tall fence
to get into a flower bed, and hanged itself.
You put down your books, pulled the stake free,
lowered the body into the weeds, went inside to
wash your hands, then waited for your mother to come home.
In the minimart, memory grotesques to reverie,
or is it speculation—one of few things
minimarts offer for free? That's not your mother.
If she were here, she'd say straighten up. That's not
your jug of milk. She'd say, Boy—
are you telling stories? Your mouth opens to speak
but you won't answer her.

Silkworms

"Somebody is in bed with somebody
In the nudie machine business"—were
Somebody's last words as the elevator lurched
To a halt. Our faces turned to mercury
In the light of phones. How dutifully
Filmed, hard at work, unaware as silkworms
In a doomed spacelab, we once were.
Our voices changed in the dark. Every
Face when we were rescued that day became
A cautionary tale in particular
Stages of bloom or wilt or burn.
In daylight, reeds shuddered where heat escaped,
We smelled the hairspray of passing children, our
Spool never stopped jarring us back to earth.

Strategic Air Command Museum

Beneath the shooting star, the dragon lady, the voodoo, the colossal peace-
maker that once teetered into flight above the Nature Theatre of Okla-
homa, we look into the vintage snarl of wiring, metal talons having long
released their quarry on cold journeys, where trained men were bent against
instruments. We're candling an egg to find our fathers in tumescent glass
turrets. My son is learning how to read and wants to see the words sten-
ciled inside. *Lift me up*— so I

lift the boy's body

into the oily dark of

open bomb bay doors.

Floating Motels

Into steel-radial freight, I call out for you, only to find spent tread of the
overpass behind a Travel Lodge, weeds we know are there in the seams. I
yell your name into the fragrance and freightliner of invasive dodder at this
sodium hour of turbines and signal towers.
                                        Arid winter, black
                                                    greasy frame around your phone's
                                cracked screen— Bakersfield.

Life Is Brief, Desire Infinite

Cheap Smokes, Estética Verónica, Payday
Loans, bulbs are missing in the chain
of lights along Thunderbird Road,
just the bare sockets of the strip, each
with a dog-eared space available sign
and phone number against dirty panes.
Press your face to the glass to see
what's inside: a green extension cord
travelling down the hall to a cup and straw.
But there's one unmarked, windowless
door at the bend in the strip mall. Pry open
the dark tavern at 1:15 p.m., where
a televised argument is blaring:
one actor is wearing a head bandage,
the other must be his daughter.
They're holding each other.   Your eyes
grope to adjust to the sports bar. Two-thirds
of the room is a vintage projection
screen television, faux-wood paneling.
Better sit down since you've walked in,
but there's no bartender. Must be
in the bathroom. Every stool
is occupied, but no one cranes to
see who walked in. The soap opera
so loud, no one could talk
if they wanted to in the spectrum washout,
light not blended enough to be called
color TV. The actors' faces
are metallic, rainbows on oily water,
but the drama plays out.
We'll get through this. She touches his face,
says *We'll be okay.* That girl is
nobody's child. None of us are.
Come with me, says the bandaged man.

Crisis Center

Through windbreak trees, snarled easement between interstate and vanish-
ing town, a girl on a bilboard, arms and hands around her pregnant belly,
hides her face from traffic. Beside her, blossoms the white daffodil of a
tornado siren and the words *you are not alone.* On an old house
                              a flaking square of
                                   grey plywood reads *ring the bell*
                         24/7.

Weekly Rates

In the mildly erotic pavilions
Of wrong questions and bountiful answers,
There is the croon of the California Zephyr
Where locomotive light thickens
The drifting snow of 3 a.m., where one
May, if one wishes, put motel furniture
Up on the tracks. A transmigration of harder
Selves, an owl spits out its pellet of bone,
Tooth, claw, leaving what's left, what you've become:
A lamp, a bed, the sharpened pencils,
Steaming cup, tidy desk, the empty chair.
You can do anything you want in that room
Filling with the light of clean surfaces.
What are you waiting for? Get up there.

Pocket Epic

The wee hour's figure hulked, clutched its bludgeon,
A pickaxe with loose handle, whose pick's flight—
O luminous path of a pickaxe at night!—
Broke the walled arteries of his foreign
Brain. The hero then vowed never to sleep again.
And as the city did as told, he told it
I love you—and it said, don't you dare say that
To me, so the hero did as told and envied the sudden
Ease of the sweat-darkened lawyers at the bar,
How they laughed among their kind. He wanted
To be in his element, to tell the joke and not
Hear the New Age pan-flute of terror.
And the city wrapped its legs around the hero's neck and
Said shut your mouth: you have no element.

Opossum

Back from the mechanic, the clinic, fuel line snipped, mouth numb,
driver's test botched, you're walking off your colonoscopy, your eye exam,
your re-failed Graduate Record Exam, warning lights throbbing, clattering
teeth in plastic tube the dentist bequeathed you, when you see its naked
tail held up from the mud, blue-black poppy pedals for ears, product of a
rushed gestation in fetid mother pouch, mangy fur stopping in its tracks,
this council with yourself its eyes now intercept, finite hierarchies of
instinct, black visors where you cannot find your own reflection anywhere,
your step crushes
                salt on sidewalk, turns
                        its head, gummy gape pierced by
                incisors, a grin.

Hilbre Island

The golf tournament where you were born, holes
where televised sea stretches out and away,
sand at the mouth of the estuary,
fingers still slip from your hands, counterfoils
as memory, glistening pools left where the tides
abandon like droplets or butterfly
eggs clustered on a gray afternoon's veiny
leaf. As if salt could draw the bitter oils
from you. You smoke with your back to us,
drinkers who think you exotic. Look away,
you're as far from the sea as continent
allows. Not far enough to ask where is
the sister who swam with you that grey day?
Now pain, then more pain, tides are like that.

Cenotaphs

Desert hardened leather, turned it
to cracked mud, filled our father's shoes with black
widow eggs, lunar orbs suspended
in webs none of us could see, where centipedes
found refuge and had to be knocked out
onto a weedy edge of pepper gardens
gone to seed and ants. As if he had
stepped out of them to walk the thorny yard
barefoot, shoes neatly paired
behind him. When he died, his cigar
smoke vanished from curtains, his shirts
given away, but shoes would wait for us
after school by a fold-up chair
toppled by wind, where weeks before,
when we were still children, he
gathered desert night around him,
lights of houses nestled in foothills, our house
at last quiet with sleepers who had no idea
of his fears for us, or why he left them to
walk away and make them our own.

FEVERSCAPE

Home

The balcony, the little chairs
and table with plastic chrysanthemum,
the window blinds mellow and from
another time. I imagined a healthy fern
inside there where someone would
press a wet washcloth to my
forehead when I didn't think I needed it
then they'd tell me you need this
and when I'd try to thank them,
shhhh this kind person would say.
It was that kind of place, you've seen it,
the narrow French doors, the balcony
peeking over a wall of oleanders.
From my booth at Denny's I watched it.
It was hard to resist the dream of trespass then,
when home thinks you're at work and
work thinks you're at home, all the while the balcony
kept whispering Marrakesh to me.
A man could smoke something elaborate
beside a dish of olives up there, so late
at night I left my carafe of decaf and waffle
and passed the parking garage and climbed its metal fence
in the hedge, hefting myself over the balcony to
look inside the French doors,
and there was a snack machine and some glossy
brochures in a rack, and I knew anyone
driving by would see me. I didn't
have much time. Then a woman
in a bathing suit came down a hallway,
and a man in a robe stepped out from a door.
It was a tanning salon, I had been looking
at the back of a tanning salon. For fear a spotlight
would be on me, I climbed back down
and tried to retrace my steps.
The parking garage was dark with its few
cars, and I felt like it was the day after

the apocalypse was supposed to happen,
a kind of shame, at intervals light fixtures
in rows reached back until I couldn't
see them. I went back to my breakfast,
which had been cleared away,
and there were strangers at my table.
Do you want your check, the assistant manager
asked me, and I said I was sorry,
that I'd left something in my car, and
that I was ready to settle up,
and he said he knew I was good for it
and laughed and that I'd be back.
He knew where to find me.

In Your Dream of Bitter Gall

The mother of the friend you left
to die by the side of the road
doesn't mind you helping yourself
to deviled eggs, or lifting the lids
of casseroles and haunting
the rooms where you had played and
planned the rest of your lives.
In no time your teeth are sinking
into hard-shelled delicacies,
and she's frying two eggs—one for you
and one for her. The glare of a half-inch
of oil in a green skillet
smears your glasses and picture frames,
keeping you from seeing
if her dead boy is married, how age
is holding him. Your swimsuit
is still folded by a sliding glass door.
When she asks you how you're getting along
you know enough to say that you have
a job now, and how proud she must be
of the son she says is a surgeon in California,
and that you've moved away, but the glare
of the oil makes you drowsy. And where's home?
You want to say you're still living somewhere
north of the Mogollon Rim, but you're
talking the geology of a place you've never lived.
You want to open your eyes,
see the shoulder of your sleeping wife, and
close them again, and say Omaha,
my wife and I live in Omaha.

Weltschmerz

Gauzy clouds flatten
above Certified Transmission,
and four necktied employees of the employee-
owned grocery store cafeteria
are eating chicken tenders
as the Japanese fire seawater
from a cannon
onto a reactor that will burn through
whatever is beneath us all.
The channel then cuts to a pep band
in straw hats sliding
trombones toward a
cheer squad with stickers
on their faces. The Kinks'
"Come Dancing" echoes over
shamrock cookies, and there must be
free refills on my soda, for workers
with full cups shuttle to and from
their tables against the bank
of windows opening onto a
butane tank padlocked in a cage.
Earlier today on my couch,
I felt the fragile weight of my
infant son as he slept
on my chest. I was so tired
I fell immediately into
a dream of a pretty nurse
buttoning up her white uniform
as if I had missed out
on the first half of my own dream,
but when she asked me what the word
Weltschmerz meant, and
when I told her it meant our unique
and individual portion of
human suffering, she cried.
Dogs began barking,

the baby twitched up crying,
strings of drool on my shirt,
and I woke to a man in my screen door
holding a clipboard, just on the other side
of my bare feet. He was
selling windows. Didn't mean to
wake the little guy, bro.
Got a minute?

Fortune Is a Door without Hinges

Yell what you want through the hole you put your money into. And the minimart's bulletproof Lazy Susan turns until your money faces the man on the other side. Now that's his money. He knows the prices with tax by heart, which are odd figures. You can't be trusted to get what you want, which could be anything stacked around him: smokes, glass pipes, batteries, pornography, ammunition, baby formula, southern comfort. He swivels in an office chair. Once, while visiting a five-hundred-year-old convent, you watched the offertory door, a Lazy Susan made of wood that turned inside a stone wall that kept the village from the nuns. Inside that opening, a little boy placed a nectarine. How the fruit glowed long after it turned and vanished. No goodbye, no have a good one, no thank you, the bulletproof Lazy Susan turns toward you until there's a quart of beer and coins. Take it. That's yours.

There is another man who also knows the prices with tax by heart, which are odd figures. At Checkmate Payday Loans, you can't be trusted to get what you want, which could be anything stacked around you all the time: smokes, batteries, baby formula, a quart of beer. Yell what you want through the hole you put your paperwork into. He swivels in an office chair. The numbers inside the lacquered wood glow long after they leave your head. No goodbye, no have a good one, the bulletproof hole turns until your payday advance waits for you. That's his money. Take it, it's yours.

Why All Music Is Folk Music

Talk radio frays to static as we drive snow-covered fields.
Entering a shelterbelt of trees, the antenna mysteriously
catches The Hebrides Overture, and the baby wakes in his car seat.
Hills blushing in sunset and in the rearview mirror,
cheeks still red from his nap and the fields, his eyes
open to Mendelssohn's ingenious reductive mechanisms,
an orrery cycling ellipses as the unscarred ice turns
charcoal, then nacre against the flipping latticework of poplars.
Tiny socked feet twitch to what he hears for the first time.

Family Memoir

Sister was tall and looked nothing like us
as she learned to dance the merengue. Her hips
did X as her legs did Y—then a step to the A to the B
to the A to the B then she vanished.
Television floated like an airship
precariously close to the rug, where geriatric spaniels
mounted each other until mother yelled stop
deflowering your brother. I mean it now quit.
Our drafty duplex screen door
blew open onto canals and tetanus
shots and vans. The goat's bladder contained
what brother thought was wine. So he slept,
but not alone, in the corrugated culvert
of sweatshirts and foam. That was when father
did time for tripwire fraud. Oh the interminable winter
we sent little brother down the crawlspace
calling him a pussy because he was totally acting like one.
We saw our breaths as we said it. Pussy.
He said a little prayer and lit the pilot light.
Plume from a blow dart was how he described it
from the ICU. A boom box at his wake
played a Madonna song telling us we lived
in a material world. We cried into our
sailor jerry. We took turns confessing
new buried trauma as the high seas of
emotional memory dreamed each of us
differently. We wrote it all down in workshops,
became lost mariners inside a grievous hull,
signing books, answering questions about sister,
who is suing us. At every podium, our readers
look at us expectantly, as if we were on
suicide watch in a cell of cordage, reliable
narrators, who have yet to survive.

The Radish Garden

Sunday morning, my father is yelling in a voice reserved for when I make mistakes, for when I feed the dog pork bones or when I leave a sprocket set scattered in the rain. *Get out here, boy. Quick.* I am barefoot, running across bullhead thorns to the chicken wire fence I had helped him build. He is bent over in the garden with his wrists in the ground. A brown radish, split and thick as his arm, is between his hands in the soil. As I run up—the soles of my feet peppered with thorns—he says, *Watch!* and pulls the fat radish from its grip.

Death—the quick taste
of a bitter and split root
left too long in the earth.

Summer, my father introduces me to his mistress, and my mother begins to bury herself in the needle work and red earth of Oak Creek Canyon. I ask him what he does when he goes to work, and two doors swing open: there, beneath powerful fans, lights, and eager young doctors, lies my first corpse—a brown man with frizzy gray hair. I am nine years old. The saw cuts through the skull like butter. My father brings the heart on a board, places his finger on spots where it has failed. *Boy, tell me what you're thinking right now.*

By a fluke, an owl
over the pitch lot—where is
the light for shadow?

In the studio of his mistress, two men share a narrow love seat with a boa constrictor coiled between their arms and necks, weaving them together in a shimmering and patterned band. Against the walls lean paintings with baffling titles: one, a green murk beneath a tuft of scrub she calls *Soldier;* another, a bloodied sliver of moon mingled with starfish, conches, and jellyfish she names *Constance.* There's no place to sit, and I grow tired under the confused paintings and try not to watch the couple wound inside the snake. The men drink milk from Pearl Beer glasses we used to have at home. *Don't tell Mama we came here*, and *What do think of the two men playing with each other? Do you like girls or boys?*

Cicadas in a storm
by the gravel road
sing infinite and brief names.

After my father's funeral, I am watering the garden and wearing Sunday
school slacks, without a shirt, socks, or shoes. I drag the hose over a shoul-
der, and ants stream from the hose onto my back and neck. They storm my
vacant shoes. I've flung a collared shirt onto the sticky leaves of the sum-
mer squash where the ants enter and exit pockets and sleeves. Their angry
ant minds are baffled by my absence. The house outside the garden fills
with people, and the strike of hard heels on distant kitchen tiles enters the
chicken wire like dust on butter beans and plants heavy with split and dull
tomatoes. I close the gate, leave the running hose to hang from the arms
of a scarecrow. The vegetables go begging on the vine.

Persimmons, pristine
and high in the tree—keepsakes
for an empty house.

Our family flies to Honduras for a wedding, and the plane rattles and sinks
into a valley of green decay, low thunderheads and ditched cars. In the
seats around me, my brothers, mother, aunts worry and hold hands. The
plane jerks and sinks, and they repeat: *we're okay, we're okay, we'll be okay...* A
stranger in the seat next to me falls apart about a baby daughter in Tulsa.
Beyond the wing approach trees for which I have no name. I take out
pictures of the family I brought to show the new in-laws. The photographs
shake in my hand: my baby face covered with sand; the brothers jump mo-
torcycles in the desert; smiles and cans of beer surround a table 1979; my
mother squints in the sun of her wedding; my father stands alone on some
Mexican shore as the light from the Sea of Cortez holds him in the frame.
His square hands cradle a gnarled head of driftwood, and as he stares
into it—the ground rising now beyond the quivering wing—his white hair
reaches out to the wind.

White cedars moan,
and a grackle on the lam
pauses for their voices.

Jeremiad

At least there's a crescent of bread in the blind brick layer's hand,
And a metallic flash down the long fuselage
Of an American Airlines MD-88, a wingéd thermos tilting out
From the trees along the river,
Vanishing into the low ceiling. With a can of beer
Stashed between his dusty boots, how can you be so sad
When you're always wrong about what you're looking at?
Its jet engines fade, and a woman giggles
In the back of a rusted church van.
The brochure she gives you reads HEAVEN OR HELL
WHICH WILL YOU CHOSE (sic)?
But this beautiful man with filthy hands will follow
Some wall or workmate's shoulder back
To a jobsite. Between collar and beatific face,
His neck is tan and vulturine. God must love
A blind working man as he eats, and you

Have been staring at him for an entire sandwich.
When he slips on a pair of reading glasses
And looks at his phone he says he doesn't need this shit.
There's an expression on his face you didn't think
Possible when he says to you, a stranger in a parking lot,
Something you can't quite hear.
Come again? you ask him, but he won't answer.

Phoenix Eclogue

I asked the man at the counter if Corona Light
came in packs bigger than twelve in the walk-in cooler.
You mean the beer cave? I doubt it. But you could look.
Need to help the people behind you. I'll meet you in there.
I pushed through the door of the walk-in
and heard a rustling like mice in grain.
And towering inside the beer cave
stood the equestrian statue of King Philip III of Spain.
It was in my way. But something tired and nimble thrashed
and stirred inside the bronze steed and monarch.
It was hard to squeeze around its forelegs
to look for Corona cases (which are a much better deal
than the twelvers). But I had to stop and admire the horse
and rider, which should be at the center
of the Plaza Mayor in Madrid, but
was now in the walk-in cooler of the Circle K
on Cave Creek and Peoria Road in Phoenix.
But what was that sound? The twitches of an insect
trapped in the inner ear? Once, my friend John
was waiting for his table at the Red Lobster
when something flew in his ear and we
had to go to the emergency room, where they
pulled out a cricket. A cricket inside a grown man's ear.
Crickets don't fly said the ER doctor. It must have been in his hair.
A little passenger, said the nurse.
I plugged and unplugged my ears. Then I
figured it out. When Giovanni de Bologna
and Pietro Tacca crafted their statue in 1616,
the horse's teeth were parted around
the monarch's bit, for the sculpted horse loved
its master's bridle. And so it was de Bologna and Tacca,
by employing the lost wax method, opened
the teeth of the metal horse in mid-piaffe,
bringing the muzzle toward its chest,
creating a lifelike aperture in the statue.
But swifts, exhausted from their trans-hemispheric

migration, took it for a nesting nook, as they do
gutters or roof tiles. Once past the teeth, the birds
lost their way and tumbled into its hollow belly.
How generations of trapped birds
had heard the flute and ankle bells of buskers and fire eaters,
or the inquisition's spectacle in the plaza. These last
remaining birds would now hear people
buying boxes of Michelob Ultra. Consider
the horse frozen in place, perennially filled
with starving swifts until now. Think of the voyage
from the tip of Africa to Plaza Mayor, how swifts sleep
in midflight, change their body temperature during storms
crossing the Mediterranean. I was thinking about this
when the clerk finally joined me. Any luck?
No, but nice statue. Pretty cool, eh?
We just put that in here for the Super Bowl.
It's from Spain. I know. Are those birds?
Yeah. They said they'd quiet down. I bet
you didn't expect to see this in here. No, I really didn't.
It's okay. No one does.

Feverscape

Lightning splits the pepper tree outside
the window, and its halves flap sparks against
power lines. The night begins in a harvest
of harlequin bugs and velvet ants where
once eggplants and chilies swelled like blisters.
Fields harbor strange cats and search lights

fanning into the empty dust. The lights
must be looking for an inmate outside
the razor wire. Tonight your blistered
body crops up in a canal against
the main spillway's rusty grates, where
river water trickles and harvesters

fling alfalfa dregs and dust— a harvest
of spores and strains of valley fever—light
enough to travel entire counties. Where
can you hide in a barren field, outside
of digging a hole into the blight? Against
the tractor leans a broken and blistered

eucalyptus. Monsoons of dust blister
the wallpaper, the witless flag, harvesting
scrub and shallow-rooted trees. Against
the dark backdrop of storm, prison lights
scour the void, and they will find you outside
chain-link, beyond aqueducts, where

vultures have begun on the mind. Where
can anyone hide in this world? Blister
beetles riddle sheets and my dreams. Outside,
the prison looks as empty as harvest.
You hear a distant alarm and tumble lightly
through search and thunder. The dog against

the house thumps a frightened tail, and against
your better judgment, you let him in. Where
would you try to run? The tree flicking light
through gauzy curtain wisps blisters
my tongue. Gusts sway the house, and a harvesting
owl drops upon a shadow's plot. Outside,

blistering holes against the blight, where
you harvest sweat and tower light,
from this gated world, you step outside.

In Your Conspiratorial Dream

Your full name in ballpoint pen on a white envelope
arrives at your mother's house with INTERPOL letterhead and
court orders from Brussels,

                                         forged dossiers,
cam feeds of you spray-painting black rectangles
across the marbled eyes of the Catholic Kings of Spain,

you cracking stained glass with a chrome tap handle
of raspberry lambic,
spooking endangered storks and so forth.

                      Now you will never become a substitute teacher.
Word spreads,
your face repeats itself across the rent-to-own centers of Kansas.

Hooligan teacher, street gang member.
                      You're under house arrest
as evidence mounts:
                camera blips of your open mouth,
dental records, an x-ray of the bottom of your feet taken from

what the pizza delivery girl in your doorway calls
                      "a tile camera in the bathroom,"
the balls of your heels peppered with primitive looking transistors
installed at your birth.

On the front lawn, a bespectacled Hungarian
masquerading as your friend Steinur takes an unnatural interest
in your hushed conversation,
                    and you and the pizza girl
suddenly race across too many boarders of tiny countries.

One hand on the wheel,
      another clutching a baffling map of tangled autoroutes
and checkpoints,
                you keep apologizing into her dashboard.
You'll straighten this out. You'll make it up to her.

In My Wifely Dream of Queens

Burdened with heraldry and helium-tight cherubim
aloft the decks and glassy bay,
her majesty's ship must sink.
Coconspirators, secret agents in her inner circle,
that we are for or against the queen
is not clear, and I'm barking orders
at you, my wife, who are wading out
with a powder keg and guttering match,
who make me promise to buy you
"new breeches when she's sunk."
We are paid hourly, and I wait
while somewhere in the kingdom, you are
secretly enjoying a private audience
with HER MAJESTY. I'm next to wade out
with powder and match. Our disguises are
terrible for swimming, even worse
for scrabbling up the slippery hull.
You're pressing hands with the queen,
turning together to somber lute music.
I'm searching the decks for newspaper,
kindling, tearing my leggings on nails.
Soon I'm the queen or myself in queenly garb
of rhinestones, faux ermine, spongy red
velvet that weighs a ton
when wet, and I'm displeased
at you, my spy staff of one, who is eating
a yellow cookie in a grocery store.
You blame the wind. My wig and white makeup
are running south, and I'm yelling
"BUT I'M THE QUEEN!"
Shoppers stop in the isles as pearls
drop from my metal lace, my spangles.
Meanwhile the real queen is proud of you.
That you press your fingers to your lips
and thank her with your mouth full of
cucumber sandwich charms Her Grace.

Winter Invective

Metal keeps cracking in the blood, bringer
of bubbling loam that freezes beneath yellow lawns,
brimming the lids of houses. And you, the blind hand
reaching in mid-slip for a hand rail
along cold steps, you broke it. You cipher.
You empty circle your unwelcomed heft
pencils in. School children in the hard chairs
they think you give them turn to stone
when you speak. A rush of air, your
voice whistles its spool of twine, and the class
is over. Rolling over the sharp objects of fever sleep,
you become a glue ball of glass bits, photographs,
home movie reels, reefs long dead and pocked,
each socket hosting its dream, memory re-fielded
with missing friend or father or a gravel drive,
foothills glittering from a chilly height,
marble pavilions they say mean yours truly
crumble while you're inside them.
Granter of paw prints, not quite an afterglow,
snow having steeped memory, ether burning off,
why say you memory maketh the man? You, shoddy
translation that you read and are. A new memory
maketh a new man (think softly sloping decline of
greenish lights, a divot where the dog
squats to maketh a steam hole, your word
spoken then revoked). In the dank interior
of a childhood dream of safety, your holes are filling in.

Video Call

As if at first metallic taste of fall
black beetle weather could decide which grief

to impose on damp air held in relief,
rain water, chimney, branch, season we call

pure, through which falls from a bird's beak to pull
one wing into elytra and be etched

into the sky's load-bearing moment's shift
away from my son's face on the phone—a shell

twitching on wet concrete. *Dada, are you
ready to disappear when I disconnect?*

One network of veins out, one is hidden
with our words dropped from the leaves to fall through

me: *I say I think so.* Now that I look
away from you, I don't know what world I'm in.

Charley

Backhoe, pitchfork, dynamite,
a second nature in my hands.
I'm no stranger, he said. To what
he was no stranger was
never clear to me. Boy, he said,
I dug the well you drink from.
Leave him alone Charley, said
the man behind the bar, and I started
writing down what Charley said. I
never looked him in the eye.
Or sat down near him. He spoke to me
across three empty barstools
at the Jackass Inn, Wilhoit, Arizona,
half past noon, the traffic of
Highway 89 breathing through
a screen door. How, when he finished
digging all the wells, the cooling tanks
for what he called the nuclear facility, he
wanted to go back to prison and
aimed his truck at a young man
in a red car. I'm gonna French kiss that boy,
he said to me. Goddammit Charley, said the barman.
I looked at my index card of Charley's words
as if I were studying a grocery list.
Punched that boy's jaw into his head
were his next words I wrote down. Charley!
And there were the canals, the
336 miles of diversion channel
from the Colorado River, all the artificial
reservoirs, water for the sixth largest city
in the country that Charley dug, and I
looked at the two inches
left of my beer, and gauged how fast
it would take me to cover
the distance between my stool and
my car outside. It was worth it,

said Charley. How he waited by
the wrecked cars to be handcuffed.
I saw his flares and sirens. Charley,
come here a minute. Charley said
the words plea bargain, and I wrote
it down. And he seemed to be
breaking up in the reentry
of his own talk. They keep calling
me to pick up my gun at the station
but I know better. Charley come over
here and help me. How he
threw something called a desert eagle
into a motel pool. Made them
swim down and fish it out. Then I
heard the screen door slam shut
and knew the barman had taken Charley
away. I waited in the empty bar
to leave, and when I pushed through
the screen door, there was Charley
on the other side of the highway,
off the shoulder in a field, a red and
black kite twice his size in his hands,
how small Charley looked, and tied
to the other end was the barman
in biker leathers unspooling twine, yelling,
back up Charley. Back up. Keep
going. That's it. Now let go.
And he did.

DERRINGER

Fly

Slaughterhouse fly on the side of a water glass, motionless in the
shadowy approach of my hand, its six bent legs, pinkish undercar-
riage, hatched in a seam of horse blood with a thousand sisters and
brothers, is the only
              child god to walk on
                    water I take with me— ice
              falling to my teeth.

Xmas Tree Farm

A child is freed from the bunker of an evil
Man, and the police commissioner,
Distracted by the press conference's orchard
Of microphones, says aren't we all, all
Of us in a bunker like a frightened child,
Isn't childhood itself a bunker, the bunker
Of childhood?—and the commissioner's future
Turns into a pasture vast and peopled

With an ex-commissioner's thoughts and not
Unlike an abandoned Xmas tree farm's brown
Dollops above a gas station that employs me
Daily. In the window, tannenbaums wait
To catch fire. I talk to the woman
Working with me, but she won't talk to me.

Headquarters

Maricopa, Arizona 1976

Huevos rancheros, hash browns, shotguns
in the truck, the promise of doves
spilled across alfalfa fields. I know why
they called it Headquarters and
why we stopped there and stayed. The bar
early in the morning was full of cowpokish truckers
and drifters, among them my father. There were
scorpions in resin for sale, mints
beneath the glass at the register, too many
sweaters for a would-be-cold-day-of no
hunting in the desert, and the bathroom
light and latch never worked. As I sat there
in the dark, my mother guarding the door
was angry at me, at my father, at the smoke.
But these were the things we could have
at the center of the world called Headquarters,
and they had them there.

Semana Santa: Procesión de Silencio

Children dressed like sailors
on their papas' shoulders
block the moon.
Hooded *penitentes* and their candles
glide by under a dark cross.

The plaza breathes
and moves their feet.
Prayers misfire in my head
as thirty flames float
through limbs and coats.

A perfumed shadow
puts a hand on my neck
and mistakes me for her husband.
"*Quédate*," she whispers,
"*Quédate quieto*."

Regret, an Index of Failed Last Lines

...a fine rain adds up.
...a frozen length of chain outside.
...an asphyxiated cup.
...and for the picking, living mere alluvium to hold them.
...an errant cloud of woodchucks—terrible eyes.
...a nightmare shot from one point of night to the other.
...as a scratch of road rising like a wick.
...as if my life were underlined in glittering foil.
...behind lashes unfolding black leaves.
...children, sleep well.
...climbing, they take certain steps to sleep.
...doves tumbling through a hole in the house.
...dust, yours. All yours.
...had I a home, a scree of lights.
...had I a wisp of fog before sunrise.
...had I conspicuous green-eyed flowers.
...moon slipping through power lines of this hometown.
...not the labored chewing of cattle.
...of birds they call strays.
...sky, out of reach, fruit ripening high in the tree.
...time, it will be our secret.
...we linger. The ferry leaves.
...where a banjo sings to the sea.
...you are still pretending to sleep.

Field

Walking rain-slogged parcels, leggy fescue tufts and drooling thatch, you are helpless as blue fiber optic lost among the grass. Green cable boxes, drizzle-slicked and obsolete tombstones, rise out of the soil as killdeers strafe notes over implacable angles, but to keep looking at the half-developed lots is to undress a carcass from memory. A rivulet of blood leaves the drain, travels back into the nostrils of a deer's warming body. The hunter's hand that holds the knife, rises to

> zip up the body,
>> eyes blinking into fear—just
> as the shot is fired.

Derringer

My grandfather puts down his beer and unwraps the oily red rag around a rim-fired, breech-loading, single-action derringer.

∿

As his thumbnail slides across the derringer's grip, he calls it polished bone. Sometimes he calls it pearl. Or mother-pearl. He tells me that it killed the president. That the derringer has the slowest bullet ever. Then he hands it to me.

∿

But on one side of the derringer, centered on the grip panel as if in a cameo brooch of yellowing resin, there floats the smallest scorpion I have ever seen. The kind that kills toddlers and the infirm. That killed the little dog named Bosley who slept under a snarl of hedges. Turn the derringer over, and there's a second scorpion. And they're real, for one's stinger is curved, the other straight.

∿

In front of adults drinking adult beverages, I point the derringer at the window, dry fire it, then turn the barrel on myself. The derringer fits perfectly in a child's hand. Hold it up, and the pale legs and stinger suspended in its grip glow against lamp light. I am on both sides of the derringer, my heart is beating, and there's no one to stop me.

∿

Give Granddaddy back his gun. It's time for bed. All night, scorpions scurry in my sheets.

∿

My grandfather quits jobs when he gets them. Takes his time coming home when he quits. Too small for a holster, the derringer can be mounted on a silver belt buckle with polished turquoise and coral, and he wears it when we go to county line liquor stores and at the dock where he lowers a crab pot into oily water by the refinery. He wears it when he mows the lawn.

∾

Once in a parking lot, the derringer falls from its buckle, shattering a side panel from its grip. This is before he loses Inez. Before strange men gather around his riding mower and easy chair. Before he dumps the contents of his wallet, then the wallet, then his clothes two stories down onto the gravel and hibiscus outside his window.

∾

He writes poems about Jesus paying his bills in heaven's grocery store. He tells me he had to fire the derringer "to shoot the lip" off a water moccasin.

∾

In a storage unit a lifetime later, I find the derringer. Through the empty frame of its grip, there's the cardboard bottom of a box, the smell of rat killer. The breach-loading latch is flimsy. The snub barrel wobbles on a wiry hinge when I look inside it. It never had a firing pin.

∾

I miss the exit home again and keep driving long after dark. There's a phone ringing in my coat. Why do you do this to yourself? Why are you doing this to me? And as I try to answer you, I can feel his hands unwrapping the oily red cloth. His fingernail pointing into the kitchen late at night, tracing the path of a bullet I can still see in midflight.

Coda: Petrichor

When rain comes   home from the counselor's small table

between our chairs   with tissues we took

turns shaking our heads   our way of breaking

each other down

breaks open   tributaries

diverge   what was it

we argued about?   so the lattice of exhausted delta

a patchwork of thunder cells   may enter our open door

there are no birds

where we had once seen them   now part of us

we cannot unlock

or salvage   breached by vapor sifting through hardpan

is here for a moment   and so are we

to receive the soil's unlatching seeds   waking grubs in chambers

our voices sated and veiled

there are the reeds   there is the sweet smell

Acknowledgments:

Beacon Street Review, Chariton Review, Clockhouse Review, Crabcreek Review, Cutbank, Exit 7, First Class Lit, Flyway, I-70 Review, Manifest West, Midwest Quarterly, Painted Bride Quarterly, The Pinch, Poetry Kanto, Sierra Nevada Review, Stand Magazine, Strange Machine, Sugar House Review, Talking River Review, and *Verve.*

Poems in this collection have also appeared in the chapbook *Afterlives,* published by Finishing Line Press, as well as in the anthology *The Narrow Chimney Reader: Volume I,* edited by Jesse Sensibar & James Jay, published by Uptown Pubhouse Press.

The author wishes to thank the following people for their help in writing this book: James Jay, Greg Kosmicki, Natalie Peeterse, and Todd Robinson.

The author also wishes to recognize The Anderson Center at Tower View, the University of Nebraska Omaha Writer's Workshop, and the University Committee on Research and Creative Activity for material support and time.

About the Author

Miles Waggener is the author of two poetry collections: *Phoenix Suites* (The Word Works, 2003), winner of the Washington Prize; and *Sky Harbor* (Pinyon Publishing, 2011); as well as the chapbooks *Portents Aside* (Two Dogs Press, 2008) and *Afterlives* (Finishing Line Press, 2013). His poems have appeared in numerous anthologies and journals including *New Poets of the American West; Verse Daily; Helen Burns Poetry Anthology: New Voices from the Academy of American Poets' University and College Prizes; Antioch Review; Cutbank; Green Mountains Review; Crazyhorse; Seneca Review;* and *Beloit Poetry Journal.* He has won individual artist fellowships from The Arizona Commission on the Arts and the Nebraska Arts Council. Since 2006, he has been a faculty member of the University of Nebraska at Omaha Writer's Workshop.